reflections *on friendship*

reflections

on friendship

compiled by Suvajra and Vidyadevi

WINDHORSE PUBLICATIONS

Published by Windhorse Publications
11 Park Road
Birmingham
B13 8AB
www.windhorsepublications.com

Cover photo Devamitra
Design Marlene Eltschig
Printed by Interprint Ltd, Marsa, Malta

A catalogue record for this book is available
from the British Library

ISBN 1 899579 29 X

contents

1 Introduction
5 Another World
6 The Heart's Counting Knows Only One
8 The Greatest of All Gifts
9 Loyal Friends
11 Friendship is Unnecessary
12 Being Visited by a Friend During Illness
13 Praising a Friend
14 Love and Friendship
15 Real Friendship
16 Why?
17 The Essence of Friendship
20 To Li Po on a Winter Day
21 To Tu Fu from Shangtung
22 Hope
23 More and More Beautiful
24 The Solidest Thing We Know
25 The Good Qualities of Our Friends
26 Trying to Create a New Life
27 A Kind of Sequel to Love
28 Mutual Utility
29 Proverb
30 True Friends
31 Delight or Pain?
32 The Good Friends of a Bodhisattva
34 A Series of Kindnesses
35 A Sense of Identity
36 An Ennobling Influence
39 Remembrance of Things Past

41 The Good Friend

42 With Kindly Eyes

44 Your Needs Answered

47 The Moon on the Path of the Stars

48 Three Qualities

49 I Hear It Was Charged Against Me

50 Two People, One Heart

51 Stellar Friendship

53 Where Should I Search?

54 The Most Satisfying Experience in the World

56 Like A Wildflower

57 Confronted with another human being

60 Contraries

61 A Letter To P'ei Ti from the Hills

63 Grace Abounding

65 A Different Species

66 Accepting the Silence

68 Lies about Love

To Vijayanandi

INTRODUCTION

'Put not your trust in princes, nor in any child of Man; for there is no help in them.'

There was a time in my life when I felt so isolated, disappointed, and mistrustful that I pinned this Bible verse on my wall with the sense that it expressed a fundamental truth about the nature of human existence. It has been a special pleasure to put together this collection of reflections on friendship, and in doing so to realize how much my attitude has changed.

For many years now I have been happy to accept the Buddha's statement that friendship is 'the whole of the spiritual life' – feeling, indeed, that it is friendship more than anything else that gives my life direction, authenticity, and joy.

For this change, I have, of course, to thank my friends. Friendship is that most precious thing, a free gift – indeed, the greatest gift bestowed on us, according to

Cicero – 'with the single exception of wisdom'. Not determined by ties of blood, by legal statute, or by economic necessity, friendship is mysterious in its arising and elusive of definition, although many people, including some of those in this collection, have sought to define it, or to explain how it may be sustained. On the other hand – to add to the mystery – Emerson calls it 'the solidest thing we know'. I have been struck by how often the writers quoted here refer to 'real friendship', as though the very essence of friendship is authenticity – which does seem to be true.

Appropriately for a collection on this theme, this book is the result of a collaboration between myself and Suvajra, a man renowned for his very evident qualities as a friend. It has been a great pleasure to work with him, and to sense his deep commitment to our theme.

Thanks also to my friends at Windhorse Publications for all their work on this small book.

May these reflections encourage us all to be better friends to our friends....

Vidyadevi

ANOTHER WORLD

Getting truly to know another human being is like exploring a new continent – or another world. One plunges into abysses, wanders among lofty mountains, is lost in the depths of mysterious forests, rests in bowers of roses with the brook sparkling beside one and the birds singing in the branches overhead, and stands on lonely shores gazing out over the illimitable expanse of sunlit waters.

Sangharakshita
Peace is a Fire

THE HEART'S COUNTING
KNOWS ONLY ONE

In Sung China,
two monks friends for sixty years
watched the geese pass.
Where are they going?,
one tested the other, who couldn't say.

That moment's silence continues.

No one will study their friendship
in the *koan*-books of insight.
No one will remember their names.

I think of them sometimes,
standing, perplexed by sadness,
goose-down sewn into their quilted
     autumn robes.

Almost swallowed by the vastness of the
     mountains,
but not yet.

As the barely audible
geese are not yet swallowed;
as even we, my love, will not entirely be
    lost.

Jane Hirshfield

THE GREATEST OF ALL GIFTS

Friendship may be defined as a complete identity of feeling about all things in heaven and earth: an identity which is strengthened by mutual goodwill and affection. With the single exception of wisdom, I am inclined to regard it as the greatest of all the gifts the gods have bestowed upon mankind.

Cicero
On The Good Life

LOYAL FRIENDS

There are these four types who can be seen to be loyal friends: the friend who is a helper is one, the friend who is the same in happy and unhappy times is one, the friend who points out what is good for you is one, and the friend who is sympathetic is one.

The helpful friend can be seen to be a loyal friend in four ways: he looks after you when you are inattentive, he looks after your possessions when you are inattentive, he is a refuge when you are afraid, and when some business is to be done he lets you have twice what you ask for.

The friend who is the same in happy and unhappy times can be seen to be a loyal friend in four ways: he tells you his secrets, he guards your secrets, he does not let you down in misfortune, he would even sacrifice his life for you.

The friend who points out what is good for you can be seen to be a loyal friend in four ways: he keeps you from wrongdoing, he supports you in doing good, he informs you of what you did not know, and he points out the path to heaven.

The sympathetic friend can be seen to be a loyal friend in four ways: he does not rejoice at your misfortune, he rejoices at your good fortune, he stops others who speak against you, and he commends others who speak in praise of you.

The Buddha
Sigalaka Sutta

FRIENDSHIP IS UNNECESSARY

*F*riendship is unnecessary, like philosophy, like art.... It has no survival value; rather it is one of those things which give value to survival.

C.S. Lewis
The Four Loves

BEING VISITED BY A FRIEND
DURING ILLNESS

I have been ill so long that I do not count
    the days;
At the southern window, evening – and
    again evening.
Sadly chirping in the grasses under my eaves
The winter sparrows morning and
    evening sing.
By an effort I rise and lean heavily on my
    bed;
Tottering I step towards the door of the
    courtyard.
By chance I meet a friend who is coming
    to see me;
Just as if I had gone specially to meet him.
They took my couch and placed it in the
    setting sun;
They spread my rug and I leaned on the
    balcony-pillar.
Tranquil talk was better than any medicine;
Gradually the feelings came back to my
    numbed heart.

Anon., trans. Arthur Waley

PRAISING A FRIEND

There are people who cannot praise a friend for the life of them. With every effort and all the goodwill in the world, they shrink from the task through a want of mental courage; as some people shudder at plunging into a cold-bath from weak nerves.

William Hazlitt

LOVE AND FRIENDSHIP

Love is like the wild rose-briar,
Friendship like the holly-tree –
The holly is dark when the rose-briar
   blooms
But which will bloom most constantly?

The wild rose-briar is sweet in the
   spring,
Its summer blossoms scent the air;
Yet wait till winter comes again
And who will call the wild-briar fair?

Then scorn the silly rose-wreath now
And deck thee with the holly's sheen,
That when December blights thy brow
He may still leave thy garland green.

Emily Brontë

REAL FRIENDSHIP

*R*eal friendship involves an awareness of the other's potential. We do not simply see what they are but what they could be.

Subhuti
Buddhism for Today

WHY?

What we ordinarily call friends and friendships are nothing but acquaintance-ships and familiarities formed by some chance or convenience, by means of which our souls are bound to each other. In the friendship I speak of, our souls mingle and blend with each other so completely that they efface the seam that joined them, and cannot find it again. If you press me to tell why I loved him, I feel that this cannot be expressed, except by answering:

Because it was he, because it was I.

Michel de Montaigne
Of Friendship

THE ESSENCE OF FRIENDSHIP

Sometimes we are more interested in someone's talents and capacities – as a bricklayer, accountant, or lecturer – than in what they are in themselves. If you are treated in this way, then, when you are no longer able or willing to employ your talents, you may have the disappointing and disillusioning experience of finding that nobody wants to know you, nobody wants to be 'friends' with you any more. We must therefore learn to see persons as persons. There must be kindness between us, there must be spiritual friendship, as there was between the Buddha and Ananda. There must be sympathy, sensitivity, and awareness.

There are two principal aspects to persons treating each other as persons. These are communication and taking delight. These two are of the essence of friendship.

Even in the case of ordinary friendship there is the great benefit and blessing of being able to share our thoughts and feelings with another human being. It has been said that self-disclosure, the making of oneself known to another human being – being known by them and knowing that you are known by them – is essential to human health and happiness. If you are shut up in yourself, without any possibility of communication with another person, you don't stay healthy or happy for long.

In the case of spiritual friendship, we share our experience of the Dharma itself. We share our enthusiasm, our inspiration, and our understanding. We even share our mistakes. Here, communication takes the form of confession.

The aspect of 'taking delight' means that we not only see a person as a person, but also *like* what we see, enjoy and take delight in what we see, just as we do with a beautiful painting or poem – except

18

that here the painting or poem is alive: the painting can speak to you, and the beautiful poem can answer back! This makes it very exciting and stimulating indeed. Here we see, we like, we love and appreciate a person entirely for their own sake, and not for the sake of anything useful that we can get out of them. This also happens in ordinary friendship to some extent, but it happens to a far greater extent in spiritual friendship – *kalyana mitrata*. The primary meaning of *kalyana* is 'beautiful'. In *spiritual* friendship we take delight in the spiritual beauty of our friend: we rejoice in his or her merits.

Sangharakshita
The Buddha's Victory

TO LI PO ON A WINTER DAY

Alone in my secluded hut,
I think of you all day, Li Po.

Whenever I read of friendship,
I remember your friendly poems.

Harsh winds tatter your old clothes
as you search for the wine of endless life.

Unable to go with you, I remember
    only
that old hermitage we'd hoped to make
    a home.

Tu Fu
trans. Sam Hamill

TO TU FU FROM SHANTUNG

You ask how I spend my time:
I nestle against a tree trunk,

listening to autumn winds
in the pines all day and night.

Shantung wine can't get me drunk.
The local poets bore me.

My thoughts head south with you,
like the Wen River, endlessly flowing.

Li Po
trans. Sam Hamill

HOPE

Your sadness is my sadness, friend, and so
When yesterday I saw you, wan with
    grief,
I yearned to give some comfort or relief,
And thus it was, the reason of your woe,
Not merely curiously, I sought to know:
Your lofty tree of sorrows, leaf by leaf
You shed upon my breast, until in brief
Space you had covered it; naught else
    could grow.
What solace could I give? Yet, sipping tea
And darkly brooding o'er the future
    years
Half an hour later, – blessed with gleams
    of mirth
And friendship strengthened, – did we
    then not see
Shine through sun, rain, like Hope
    through smiles and tears,
The sev'n-hued rainbow spanning
    Heav'n and Earth?

Sangharakshita

MORE AND MORE BEAUTIFUL

Increasingly I realize that as a friendship with someone deepens, I perceive them as more and more beautiful. Beauty is something big. It includes shadow and light, heights and depths, strength and weakness. It touches on something timeless.

I experience myself sometimes, in communication with a friend, as beautiful; beautiful in my being, beautiful on some level on which I am more than I ever thought I was.

Vidyasri
Dakini

THE SOLIDEST THING WE KNOW

I do not wish to treat friendships daintily, but with roughest courage. When they are real, they are not glass threads or frost-work, but the solidest thing we know. For now, after so many ages of experience, what do we know of nature, or of ourselves? Not one step has man taken toward the solution of the problem of his destiny. In one condemnation of folly stand the whole universe of men. But the sweet sincerity of joy and peace, which I draw from this alliance with my brother's soul, is the nut itself whereof all nature and all thought is but the husk and shell. Happy is the house that shelters a friend! It might well be built, like a festal bower or arch, to entertain him a single day. Happier, if he knows the solemnity of that relation, and honour its laws! It is no idle band, no holyday engagement.

Ralph Waldo Emerson
Friendship

THE GOOD QUALITIES
OF OUR FRIENDS

*I*t should be a part of our private ritual to devote a quarter of an hour every day to the enumeration of the good qualities of our friends. When we are not *active*, we fall back idly upon defects, even of those whom we most love.

Mark Rutherford
Last Pages from a Journal

TRYING TO CREATE A NEW LIFE

I want relations which are not purely personal, based on purely personal qualities; but relations based upon some unanimous accord in truth or belief, and a harmony of *purpose*, rather than of personality. I am weary of personality.... Let us be easy and impersonal, not forever fingering over our own souls, and the souls of our acquaintances, but trying to create a new life, a new common life, a new complete tree of life from the roots that are within us.

D.H. Lawrence
letter to Katherine Mansfield,
12 December 1915

A KIND OF SEQUEL TO LOVE

There is, of course, here and there on this terrestrial sphere a kind of sequel to love, in which that covetous longing of two persons for one another has yielded to a new desire and covetousness, to a *common*, higher thirst for a superior ideal standing above them: but who knows this love? Who has experienced it? Its right name is *friendship*.

Nietzsche
The Joyful Wisdom

MUTUAL UTILITY

There is ... the assertion that friendships should be cultivated not for the sake of kindly and affectionate feeling at all, but solely for purposes of mutual utility.... What a peculiar philosophy! People who propound this sort of theory seem to me to be doing nothing less than tearing the very sun out of the heavens. For they are, in fact, depriving life of friendship, which is the noblest and most delightful of all the gifts the gods have given to mankind.

Cicero
On The Good Life

PROVERB

The bird a nest, the spider a web, man friendship.

William Blake
Proverbs of Hell

TRUE FRIENDS

A long time ago in China there were two friends, one who played the harp skilfully and one who listened skilfully.

When the one played or sang about a mountain, the other would say: 'I can see the mountain before us.'

When the one played about water, the listener would exclaim: 'Here is the running stream!'

But the listener fell sick and died. The first friend cut the strings of his harp and never played again. Since that time the cutting of harp strings has always been a sign of intimate friendship.

Zen Flesh, Zen Bones

DELIGHT OR PAIN?

Are Friends Delight or Pain?
Could Bounty but remain
Riches were good –

But if they only stay
Ampler to fly away
Riches are sad.

Emily Dickinson

THE GOOD FRIENDS
OF A BODHISATTVA

A Bodhisattva who has set out with earnest intention and wants to win full enlightenment should from the very beginning tend, love and honour the good friends.

Subhuti: Who are those good friends of a Bodhisattva?

The Lord: The Buddhas and Lords, and also the irreversible Bodhisattvas who are skilful in the Bodhisattva-course, and who instruct and admonish him in the perfections, who demonstrate and expound the perfection of wisdom. The perfection of wisdom in particular should be regarded as a Bodhisattva's good friend. All the six perfections [giving, morality, patience, vigour, concentration, wisdom], in fact, are the good friends of a Bodhisattva. They are his Teacher, his path, his light, his torch, his illumination, his shelter, his refuge, his place of rest, his final relief, his island, his mother, his father, and they lead him to cognition, to understanding, to full enlightenment.

The Perfection of Wisdom
in Eight Thousand Lines

A SERIES OF KINDNESSES

We cannot tell the precise moment when friendship is formed. As in filling a vessel drop by drop, there is at last a drop which makes it run over; so in a series of kindnesses there is at last one which makes the heart run over.

Samuel Johnson
quoted by James Boswell in
The Life of Samuel Johnson

A SENSE OF IDENTITY

*I*n 'The Pillow and the Key' Robert Bly tells the story of a young male friend of his who had mainly female friends, whom he appreciated very much, at school, college, and work. However, he has a dream that he is living in the forest with a clan of she-wolves. One day they all run to a river bank. When they look into the river all the she-wolves are reflected, but the young man is not. Bly suggests that male companionship produces a 'face' for men. I would say that this is true for women also. Our friendships with one another give us a face, a sense of identity; we are reflected back to ourselves, as women amongst women.

Dhammadinna
in *The Moon and Flowers*

AN ENNOBLING INFLUENCE

*T*rue and genuine friendship presupposes a strong sympathy with the weal and woe of another — purely objective in its character and quite disinterested; and this in its turn means an absolute identification of self with the object of friendship. The egoism of human nature is so strongly antagonistic to any such sympathy, that true friendship belongs to that class of things — the sea serpent, for instance — with regard to which no one knows whether they are fabulous or really exist somewhere or other.

Still, in many cases, there is a grain of true and genuine friendship in the relations of man to man, though generally, of course, some secret personal interest is at the bottom of them — some one among the many forms that selfishness can take. But in a world where all is imperfect, this grain of true feeling is such an ennobling influence that it gives some warrant for calling those relations by the name of friendship, for they stand far above the ordinary friendships that prevail amongst mankind. The latter are so constituted that, were you to hear how your dear friends speak of you behind your back, you would never say another word to them.

With the ancients *friendship* was one of the chief elements in morality. But friendship is only limitation and partiality; it is the restriction to one individual of what is the due of all mankind, namely, the recognition that a man's own nature and that of mankind are identical. At most it is a compromise between this recognition and selfishness.

I observed once to Goethe, in complaining of the illusion and vanity of life, that when a friend is with us we do not think the same of him as when he is away. He replied: 'Yes! because the absent friend is yourself, and he exists only in your head; whereas the friend who is present has an individuality of his own, and moves according to laws of his own; which cannot always be in accordance with those which you form for yourself.'

Arthur Schopenhauer
Parerga and Paralipomena

REMEMBRANCE
OF THINGS PAST

When to the Sessions of sweet silent
    thought,
I summon up remembrance of things
    past,
I sigh the lack of many a thing I sought,
And with old woes new wail my dear
    time's waste:
Then can I drown an eye (unused to
    flow)
For precious friends hid in death's
    dateless night,
And weep afresh love's long since
    cancelled woe,
And moan th'expense of many a
    vanished sight.
Then can I grieve at grievances
    foregone,
And heavily from woe to woe tell o'er
The sad account of fore-bemoaned
    moan,

Which I new pay, as if not paid before.
    But if the while I think on thee (dear
       friend)
    All losses are restored, and sorrows end.

William Shakespeare
Sonnet 30

THE GOOD FRIEND

Like a compassionate mother, the good friend gives you birth into the Buddha's family. Like a compassionate father, the good friend gives benefits through his unending actions. Like a guardian, the good friend helps you in avoiding all evil. Like a great teacher, the good friend instructs you in the Bodhisattva practice. Like a guide, the good friend brings you to the other shore. Like a doctor, the good friend cures your pains from all distress. Like the Himalayan mountains, the good friend nurtures you as the mountain nurtures the plants located on them. Like a general, the good friend protects you from all fears. Like a boat, the good friend carries you across the sea of life and death. And like a boatman, the good friend helps you reach the jewelled stream of omniscience.

Avatamsaka Sutra

'I hope, Anuruddha, that you are all living in concord, with mutual appreciation, without disputing, blending like milk and water, viewing each other with kindly eyes.'

'Surely, venerable sir, we are living in concord, with mutual appreciation, without disputing, blending like milk and water, viewing each other with kindly eyes.'

'But, Anuruddha, how do you live thus?'

'Venerable sir, as to that, I think thus: "It is a gain for me, it is a great gain for me that I am living with such companions in the holy life." I maintain bodily acts of loving-kindness towards these venerable ones both openly and privately; I maintain verbal acts of loving-kindness towards them both openly and privately; I maintain mental acts of loving-kindness towards them both openly and privately.

I consider: 'Why should I not set aside what I wish to do and do what these venerable ones wish to do?' Then I set aside what I wish to do and do what these venerable ones wish to do. We are different in body, venerable sir, but one in mind.'

The Buddha and Anuruddha
Upakkilesa Sutta

YOUR NEEDS ANSWERED

And a youth said, Speak to us of
    Friendship.
And he answered, saying:
Your friend is your needs answered.
He is your field which you sow with
    love and reap with thanksgiving.
And he is your board and your fireside.
For you come to him with your hunger,
    and you seek him for peace.

When your friend speaks his mind you
    fear not the 'nay' in your own mind,
    nor do you withhold the 'ay'.
And when he is silent your heart ceases
    not to listen to his heart;
For without words, in friendship, all
    thoughts, all desires, all expectations
    are born and shared, with joy that is
    unacclaimed.

When you part from your friend, you
    grieve not;

For that which you love most in him
   may be clearer in his absence, as the
   mountain to the climber is clearer
   from the plain.
And let there be no purpose in friendship save the deepening of the spirit.
For love that seeks aught but the
   disclosure of its own mystery is not
   love but a net cast forth: and only the
   unprofitable is caught.

And let your best be for your friend.
If he must know the ebb of your tide, let
   him know its flood also.
For what is your friend that you should
   seek him with hours to kill?
Seek him always with hours to live.
For it is his to fill your need, but not
   your emptiness.
And in the sweetness of friendship let
   there be laughter, and sharing of
   pleasures.

For in the dew of little things the heart
finds its morning and is refreshed.

Kahlil Gibran
The Prophet

THE MOON
ON THE PATH OF THE STARS

Rely on the noble, the spiritual, the steady; the learned, the prudent, the wise. One wise enough to follow such beings is like the moon on the path of the stars.

Dhammapada

THREE QUALITIES

One who is endowed with three qualities is a friend to be followed. What are these three qualities? Giving what is difficult to give, doing what is difficult to do, forgiving what is difficult to forgive.

The Buddha
Anguttara-Nikaya i.286

I HEAR IT WAS CHARGED
AGAINST ME

I hear it was charged against me that I
 sought to destroy institutions,
But really I am neither for nor against
 institutions,
(What indeed have I in common with
 them? or what with the destruction of
 them?)
Only I will establish in the Mannahatta
 and in every city of these States inland
 and seaboard,
And in the fields and woods, and above
 every keel little or large that dents the
 water,
Without edifices or rules or trustees or
 any argument,
The institution of the dear love of
 comrades.

Walt Whitman
Leaves of Grass

TWO PEOPLE, ONE HEART

Singing waka, reciting poems, playing ball
            together in the fields –
Two people, one heart.

Ryokan
trans. John Stevens

STELLAR FRIENDSHIP

We were friends, and have become strangers to each other. But this is as it ought to be, and we do not want either to conceal or obscure the fact, as if we had to be ashamed of it. We are two ships, each of which has its goal and its course; we may, to be sure, cross one another in our paths, and celebrate a feast together as we did before, – and then the gallant ships lay quietly in one harbour and in one sun-shine, so that it might have been thought they were already at their goal, and that they had had one goal. But then the almighty strength of our tasks forced us apart once more into different seas and into different zones, and perhaps we shall never see one another again, – or perhaps we may see one another, but not know one another again; the different seas and suns have altered us! That we had to become strangers to one another is the law to which we are *subject:* just by that

51

shall we become more sacred to one another! Just by that shall the thought of our former friendship become holier! There is probably some immense, invisible curve and stellar orbit in which our courses and goals, so widely different, may be *comprehended* as small stages of the way, – let us raise ourselves to this thought! But our life is too short, and our power of vision too limited for us to be more than friends in the sense of that sublime possibility. – And so we will *believe* in our stellar friendship, though we should have to be terrestrial enemies to one another.

Friedrich Nietzsche
The Joyful Wisdom

WHERE SHOULD I SEARCH?

Sudhana looked up to the sky and said, 'Bravo, O noble one, sympathetic one; you are trying to help me and show me spiritual friends. Tell me, in the right way, how to proceed; where should I go? Where should I search? What should I meditate on to see spiritual friends?'

The supernatural being said, 'One may go into the presence of spiritual friends by an attitude of universal respect, by mental focus on remembering spiritual friends in all things, by concentration speeding everywhere by dreamlike speed of mind, by realizing mind and body as like reflections.'

Avatamsaka Sutra

THE MOST SATISFYING
EXPERIENCE IN THE WORLD

*I*t is the most satisfying experience in the world to have someone you can speak to as freely as your own self about any and every subject upon earth. If things are going well, you cannot possibly enjoy your prosperity to the full unless you have another person whose pleasure equals your own. Should things go wrong, your misfortunes will indeed be hard to bear without someone who suffers as badly as yourself, or even worse....

Friendship, then, both adds a brighter glow to prosperity and relieves adversity by dividing and sharing the burden.... It is unique because of the bright rays of hope it projects into the future: it never allows the spirit to falter or fall. When a man thinks of a true friend, he is looking at himself in the mirror. Even when a friend is absent, he is present all the same. However poor he is, he is rich: however weak, he is strong. And may I attempt to convey an even more difficult concept? Even when he is dead, he is still alive. He is alive because his friends still cherish him, and remember him, and long for him. This means that there is happiness even in his death – he ennobles the existences of those who are left behind.

Cicero
On The Good Life

LIKE A WILDFLOWER

I am already kindly disposed towards you. My friendship it is not in my power to give: this is a gift which no man can make, it is not in our own power: a sound and healthy friendship is the growth of time and circumstance, it will spring up and thrive like a wildflower when these favour, and when they do not, it is in vain to look for it.

William Wordsworth
letter to Thomas de Quincey,
29 July 1803

CONFRONTED WITH ANOTHER HUMAN BEING

All men are but teeth on a comb' is an old Arabic saying and so it was with us. Both of us had gone through experiences that opened up new definitions of what we were as humans. But to be truly humanized and to be truly whole again it would be necessary to expose that, to share it honestly with another person. Would this man be frightened of what I thought? We become our meaningful selves only if people receive meaning from us. I doubted suddenly if I could draw from those dark days in isolation a meaning that someone would receive and understand.

Now confronted with another human being who looked at me and observed me as I did him, I found myself wondering whether I was more frightened of my friend than I was of the men who held me and who might if they so desired end my life. As much as companionship filled me with a sense of joy it was an

unresolved joy. I wanted to wash my con-
science and my memory clean from the
experience that had overpowered them
and had in some way contaminated them.
Dare I expose the scars of this outrage,
and acknowledge my own ignominy? It
might, I thought, be a kind of capitula-
tion. So much of our experience had
been dehumanizing. Would the confession of it make me permanently non-
human? A part-formed creature?

Fear of self and fear of the other re-
emerged as the constant undercurrent of
our first days together. But if there was a
gulf between us, our sense of mutual
gratitude obscured it. Faced with the
liberty we received from one another, we
cast off our sense of loss, and of atrophy.
The gregarious character which is part of
what we are as humans slowly returned to
us. We needed someone to share our
beliefs, or even lack of them. This man,

who might have been an ideological opponent forcing me to withdraw and become hostile and defensive, instead reached out to embrace as we all need and ultimately must do. But the breaking down of these fears, of these insecurities, of all this self-questioning was not an immediate thing. It takes a long time to come back to yourself. It needs a commitment to the courage of another person in order to approach them, be honest with them and know that you will not be shunned or rejected by them. That coming together over the long months and the years that lay ahead was the remaking of humanity and the re-creation of a meaningful future that seemed to have been stolen from us.

Brian Keenan
An Evil Cradling
(describing the first few days of his shared
captivity with John McCarthy)

CONTRARIES

For you the restless ocean,
For me the rocky isle;
For you the fluid manner,
For me the chiselled style.

For you mercurial passion,
For me crystálline thought;
For you the blithe 'I want to',
For me the grave 'I ought'.

Meeting at the shoreline
Where stone is ground to sand
And foam sucked into shingle
We wander hand in hand.

Sangharakshita

A LETTER TO P'EI TI
FROM THE HILLS

This twelfth month the weather has been bright and agreeable, and I could have come over the mountain, but I hesitated to disturb you, deep as you are in the Classics. So I went off for a walk in the hills. I rested at the Kanp'ei Temple, where I had something to eat with the hill monks, before I left and went north over the Black Water. The clear moon lit up all the country. In the night I went up Huatzu Hill, and the waters of the Wang River were rippling up and down with the moon. Distant lights in the cold hills were coming and going beyond the woods. The barking of the winter dogs in the deep lanes sounded like leopards. The pounding of grain in the village could be heard between the strokes of a distant bell. Now I am sitting by myself. The servants are asleep. I am thinking a lot about old days, our composing poems as we walked arm in arm along steep paths beside clear streams.

We must wait for the spring, when all the grasses and trees will come out again and we can look at the spring hills. The light dace coming out of the water. The gulls soaring. Dew wetting the green banks. The morning call of the pheasants in the corn. All this is not far off, and then you can surely come and wander about with me? If it weren't for your natural genius, I would of course not impose anything so inessential on you. But it holds deep interest. No urgency. This goes to you by a hillman. No more now.

From Wang Wei, man of the hills.

Wang Wei

GRACE ABOUNDING

Air crowds into my cell so considerately
that the jailer forgets this kind of gift
and thinks I'm alone. Such unnoticed
   largesse
smuggled by day floods over me,
or here come grass, turns in the road,
a branch or stone significantly strewn
where it wouldn't need to be.

Such times abide for a pilgrim, who all
   through
a story or a life may live in grace, that
   blind
benevolent side of even the fiercest
   world,
and might – even in oppression or
   neglect –
not care if it's friend or enemy, caught
   up
in a dance where no one feels need or
   fear:

I'm saved in this big world by
    unforeseen
friends, or times when only a glance
from a passenger beside me, or just the
    tired
branch of a willow inclining toward
    earth,
may teach me how to join earth and sky.

William Stafford

A DIFFERENT SPECIES

*I*t is well that there is no one without a
fault; for he would not have a friend in
the world. He would seem to belong to a
different species.

William Hazlitt

ACCEPTING THE SILENCE

e've been at the ranch five days now, and the days have taken on a rhythm of their own. We read in the morning, and if something occurs to us, we write a little. We march down the road to the creek like soldiers on a mission. We spend the heat of the day there throwing rocks, discussing fracture lines and strategies, getting soaked. We walk home satisfied, take turns in the claw-footed bathtub, cook something fresh and delicious to eat.

The strangest part of all this is that we've almost stopped speaking. It's not because we are mad, or even because we've run out of things to say to each other. It's something far better than that.

It's as though the snowmelt and the lengthening days have simply taken hold of us. As though we have tacitly agreed to accept the silence the mountains demand in this silent season. Summer is the time for talking, the mountains say, when the birds are singing and the creek is gurgling and there are leaves on the trees that will rustle in the wind. Now is the time to sit silently together, to feel the ice break around you, to wait for the first bluebirds to return to the feeder; now is the time to heal.

Pam Houston
A Rough Guide to the Heart

LIES ABOUT LOVE

We are all liars, because
the truth of yesterday becomes a lie
    tomorrow,
whereas letters are fixed,
and we live by the letter of truth.

The love I feel for my friend, this year,
is different from the love I felt last year.
If it were not so, it would be a lie.
Yet we reiterate love! love!
as if it were coin with a fixed value
instead of a flower that dies, and opens
    a different bud.

D.H. Lawrence

The publishers wish to acknowledge with gratitude
permission to quote from the following:

p.6: 'The Heart's Counting Knows Only One' by Jane
Hirshfield, from *The Lives of the Heart*, HarperCollins,
1997. © 1997 Jane Hirshfield. Used by permission of
the author.

p.8, p.28, p.54:
from *On the Good Life*, by Cicero, translated by
Michael Grant, Penguin Classics, Harmondsworth,
1971, pp.187, 188, 201, copyright © translation,
introduction, and notes, Michael Grant Publications
Ltd., 1971. Reproduced by permission of Penguin
Books Ltd.

p.9: © Maurice Walshe 1987, 1995. Reprinted from *The
Long Discourses of the Buddha: A Translation of the Digha
Nikaya*, with permission of Wisdom Publications,
199 Elm St., Somerville MA02144 USA,
www.wisdompubs.org

p.11: from *The Four Loves* by C.S.Lewis copyright © C.S.
Lewis Pte. Ltd. 1960. Extract reprinted by permission.
Excerpts from *The Four Loves* by C.S.Lewis, copyright
© 1960 by Helen Joy Lewis and renewed 1988 by
Arthur Owen Barfield, reprinted by permission of
Harcourt, Inc.

p.12: from Arthur Waley, *Chinese Poems*, Unwin Paperbacks,
1982. Reprinted by permission of the Arthur Waley
Estate.

p.15: from Subhuti, *Buddhism For Today*, Windhorse, 1983.

p.16: from Montaigne, *The Complete Essays of Montaigne*, trans. Donald M. Frame, Stanford University Press.

p.20, p.21:
from *Endless River, Li Po and Tu Fu: A Friendship in Poetry*, trans. Sam Hamill, Inklings, Weatherhill Inc., 1993.

p.23: from *Dakini 6*, 1990, reprinted by kind permission of Vidyasri.

p.30: from Paul Reps, *Zen Flesh Zen Bones*, Charles E. Tuttle Co. Inc., Boston and Tokyo.

p.32: from Edward Conze (trans.), *The Perfection of Wisdom in Eight Thousand Lines and Its Verse Summary*, Four Seasons Foundation, 1995.

p.35: from Kalyanavaca (ed.), *The Moon and Flowers*, Windhorse, 1997, reprinted by kind permission of Dhammadinna.

p.42: © Bhikkhu Bodhi 1995. Reprinted from *The Middle Length Discourses of the Buddha: A New Translation of the Majjhima Nikaya*, with permission of Wisdom Publications, 199 Elm St., Somerville, MA 02144, USA, www.wisdompubs.org

p.44: from Kahlil Gibran, *The Prophet*, Studio Editions, London 1995. Authorization granted by Gibran National Committee, PO Box 116-5487, Beirut, Lebanon; fax:(+961-1)396916; e-mail: k.gibran@cyberia.net.lb

p.47: from the *Dhammapada*, translated into Tibetan from the Pali by dGe-dun Chos-'phel, translated into English from the Tibetan by Dharma Publishing staff, Dharma Publishing, Berkeley, 1985.

acknowledgements

p.50: from John Stevens (trans. and introduction), *One Robe, One Bowl: The Zen Poetry of Ryokan*, Weatherhill Inc., 1977.

p.53: from Thomas Cleary (trans.), *The Flower Ornament Scripture*. © 1984, 1986, 1987, 1989, 1993 by Thomas Cleary. Reproduced by arrangement with Shambhala Publications, Inc., Boston, www.shambhala.com

p.57: from Brian Keenan, *An Evil Cradling*, Hutchinson, 1992. Reprinted with the kind permission of Brian Keenan.

p.61: *Wang Wei: Poems*, translated by G.W. Robinson (Penguin Classics, Harmondsworth, 1973) p.141, copyright © G.W. Robinson, 1973. Reproduced by permission of Penguin Books Ltd.

p.63: 'Grace Abounding' is reprinted with the permission of Confluence Press from *Even in Quiet Places*. Copyright 1996 William Stafford.

p.66: from Pam Houston, *A Rough Guide to the Heart*, Virago Press, London 2000, © Pam Houston. Also published in North America under the title *A Little More About Me*, © 1999 Pam Houston. Reprinted with the permission of Virago Press and W.W. Norton.

p.27, p.51:

from Friedrich Nietzsche, *Joyful Wisdom*, trans. Thomas Common, with an Introduction by Kurt F. Reinhardt, originally published by Frederick Ungar Publishing Co., New York, and Constable & Co. Ltd, London, 1960.

p.36: from Arthur Schopenhauer, 'Parerga and Paralipomena' (originally published in 1851 by Unwin Hyman Academics) in *The Oxford Book of Friendship*, chosen and edited by D.J. Enright and David Rawlinson, published by Oxford University Press, 1991.

p.41: from Diana Y. Paul, *Women in Buddhism, Images of the Feminine in Mahayana Tradition*, Asian Humanities Press.

The Windhorse symbolizes the energy of the enlightened mind carrying the Three Jewels – the Buddha, the Dharma, and the Sangha – to all sentient beings. Buddhism is one of the fastest-growing spiritual traditions in the Western world. Throughout its 2,500-year history, it has always succeeded in adapting its mode of expression to suit whatever culture it has encountered.

WINDHORSE PUBLICATIONS aims to continue this tradition as Buddhism comes to the West. Today's Westerners are heirs to the entire Buddhist tradition, free to draw instruction and inspiration from all the many schools and branches. Windhorse publishes works by authors who not only understand the Buddhist tradition but are also familiar with Western culture and the Western mind. Manuscripts welcome.

For orders and catalogues contact

WINDHORSE PUBLICATIONS	WINDHORSE BOOKS	WEATHERHILL INC
11 Park Road Birmingham B13 8AB UK	P.O. Box 574 Newtown NSW 2042 Australia	41 Monroe Turnpike Trumbull CT 06611 USA

Windhorse Publications is an arm of the FRIENDS OF THE WESTERN BUDDHIST ORDER, which has more than sixty centres on five continents. Through these centres, members of the Western Buddhist Order offer regular programmes of events for the general public and for more experienced students. These include meditation classes, public talks, study on Buddhist themes and texts, and 'bodywork' classes such as t'ai chi, yoga, and massage. The FWBO also runs several retreat centres and the Karuna Trust, a fund-raising charity that supports social welfare projects in the slums and villages of India. Many FWBO centres have residential spiritual communities and ethical businesses associated with them. Arts activities are encouraged too, as is the development of strong bonds of friendship between people who share the same ideals.

In this way the FWBO is developing a unique approach to Buddhism, not simply as a set of techniques, less still as an exotic cultural interest, but as a creatively directed way of life for people living in the modern world. If you would like more information about the FWBO please visit our website at www.fwbo.org

or write to

London Buddhist Centre
51 Roman Road
London
E2 0HU, UK

Aryaloka
Heartwood Circle
Newmarket
NH 03857, USA

ALSO FROM WINDHORSE

Compiled by Vidyadevi
REFLECTIONS ON SOLITUDE

Throughout the ages seekers after truth have spoken of the benefits of solitude for reflection, self-examination, and a deeper understanding of life.

This diverse and thoughtful selection of poetry and prose draws on the riches of Western literature as well as the wisdom of the Buddhist tradition, depicting the many delights and challenges of being alone.

Spend a little time with these reflections when life is crowding in on you and find some space....

80 pages
ISBN 1 899579 28 1
£4.99/$9.95

Compiled by Vidyadevi
REFLECTIONS ON WILDNESS

Wildness. The word evokes open spaces and
open hearts. Wildness is about going beyond
what the world conventionally requires,
touching the mythic dimension of life.

This imaginative and thought-provoking selection draws on the riches of Western
literature as well as the wisdom of the
Buddhist tradition. It will give you something
to dwell on – and dream about.

Don't settle for tame pleasures. Try wildness.

80 pages
ISBN 1 899579 34 6
£4.99/$9.95

Sangharakshita
THE CALL OF THE FOREST
AND OTHER POEMS

Profound contemplation of nature and
spiritual vision feature prominently in this
collection of Sangharakshita's recent poems.
Here we can see how the practice of
Buddhism combines with the writing of
poetry. Both require the cultivation of an
intense sympathy with others, which forms
the basis of the essential Buddhist virtue of
loving-kindness.

56 pages
ISBN 1 899579 24 9
£7.99/$15.95